TRUTH FOR ALL TIME

Matthias

TRUTH FOR ALL TIME

A Brief Outline of the Christian Faith

John Calvin

Translated from the French by
Stuart Olyott

THE BANNER OF TRUTH TRUST

THE BANNER OF TRUTH TRUST

3 Murrayfield Road, Edinburgh EH12 6EL
P.O. Box 621, Carlisle, PA 17013, USA

*

First published in French as
Brève Instruction chrétienne in 1537

© Stuart Olyott 1998
First Banner of Truth edition 1998
Reprinted 2000
Reprinted 2013
Reprinted 2016

ISBN 978 0 85151 749 0

*

Typeset in 11/14 pt Sabon Oldstyle
at The Banner of Truth Trust, Edinburgh

Printed in the USA by
Versa Press, Inc.
Peoria, IL

Contents

You have in your hands a small but priceless jewel. It has lain buried and forgotten for far too long, but now that it has been unearthed you will find that it shines as brightly as ever and has lost none of its value.

John Calvin knew that if the biblical truths rediscovered at the Reformation were to spread throughout the world, they would have to be presented in a form which ordinary people could understand. So, during the winter of 1536–1537, the 29-year-old Calvin wrote, in French, his *Brief Outline of the Christian Faith* [*Brève Instruction chrétienne*]. This short book is, in fact, a résumé of the first edition of his *Institutes of the Christian Religion* and many passages in it are taken word for word from that earlier work.

This *Brief Outline* was replaced in 1542 by a catechism, in which the basic doctrines were treated equally thoroughly, but in a different order. This soon became the definitive catechism of French-speaking Reformed churches throughout Europe. The renown of Calvin's catechism meant that his *Brief Outline* fell into disuse and became entirely forgotten for over three hundred years.

In 1877 an original copy, possibly the only one surviving, was discovered in the Paris National Library by Monsieur Henri Bordier. This led to the republication of the book in 1878. Translations into German (1880 and 1926) and Italian (1935) followed. A version in contemporary French was prepared by Pierre Courthial and published in 1953. It is from Dr. Courthial's modernised text and with his permission, for which I am grateful, that this English version has been translated.

As far as I know, Calvin's *Brief Outline* has appeared in English only once before. In 1949, Lutterworth Press, London, published an edition translated by Paul T. Fuhrmann. This scholarly work, which has a historical foreword and many critical and explanatory notes, closely follows Calvin's French text of 1537, as well as taking into account his own translation of it into Latin made in 1538 'for the other churches'. I have consulted this translation at every point, although I have not felt free to agree with many of its renderings.

The present translation has been checked by Carol Chapman of the Department of French in the University of Liverpool and, independently, by Margaret Lang of the Department of French in the University of Edinburgh. I am grateful to these two busy ladies for the time and care that they spent in this work. In addition to their corrections, they made very many helpful suggestions for improving the translation, most of which I have incorporated. This said, I must stress that final responsibility for the integrity and accuracy of this translation rests with me alone.

It was not Calvin's habit to give precise references for the passages of Scripture to which he alludes. These have been added to the present edition for the convenience of modern readers. You will also notice that some of Calvin's Scripture quotations are very different indeed from the renderings given by our English Bibles. This is usually because he is giving his own translation, although sometimes he is quoting from versions generally unknown to Christians today.

So here is Calvin's striking but concise attempt to define the Christian faith for ordinary people! Its aim is not to attack any person or institution, but to build up believers. Its style, though noble, is simple and uncluttered. Its matter is majestic, being soaked through with the wholesome teaching of the Holy Scriptures. Here you see the thrust and power of the early days of the Reformation. Here you have the very core of Protestant belief and feel the warmth of its ardent love for God and men.

As you read this book you will sense that the truth of God, so clearly taught here, is something that you are expected to *live*. May this be the experience of every reader who, by reading this book, is looking at the Christian faith for the first time. And may this increasingly be the experience of all of us who, by God's kindness, have already been brought into personal union with our Lord Jesus Christ.

STUART OLYOTT

Like newborn babes, desire the milk
which is both reasonable and pure.

Be always ready to answer
whoever asks you to account for the hope
which is in you.

If anyone speaks, let him speak
the words of God.

(*1 Pet.* 2:2; 3:15; 4:11).

I

Knowing God
and knowing ourselves

1. All men live in order that they might know God

You cannot find a man anywhere, however un-civilised or wild, who is without some idea of religion. This is because we have all been created to know the majesty of our Creator and, in knowing it, to think more highly of it than anything else. We are to honour it with all awe, love and reverence.

Unbelievers seek only to wipe out all memory of this sense of God which is planted in their hearts. Leaving them aside, we who claim to have a personal religion must call to mind that this present life will not last and will soon be over. We should spend it thinking about immortality.

Now, eternal and immortal life can be found nowhere except in God. It follows, then, that the main care and concern of our life should be to seek God. We should long for him with all the affection of our hearts, and not find rest and peace anywhere except in him alone.

2. *The difference between true and false religion*

It is commonly agreed that to live without religion is to live in real misery and to be in no way better than wild animals. This being so, no one will want to be considered as being entirely indifferent to personal religion and the knowledge of God.

But there are many differences in the visible form that religion takes. This is because the majority of men are not really affected by the fear of God. Nonetheless, willingly or not, they cannot escape from the idea that there is some divine being whose power either holds them up or brings them down. This idea keeps coming back to their minds. Struck by the thought of such a great power, in one way or another they revere it. This is to avoid having too great a contempt for it, for fear of provoking it to act against them. However, living in a disorderly way and rejecting all honesty, they exhibit an obvious lack of concern in the way they disregard the judgment of God.

In addition, because their estimate of God is governed by the foolish and thoughtless conceit of their own mind, and not by his infinite majesty, they actually turn away from the true God. This is why, even when they make real and careful efforts to serve God, it turns out to be a waste of time. It is not the eternal God they are worshipping, but rather the dreams and illusions of their own hearts.

Now there is a fear which would most willingly flee from the judgment of God but which, being unable to do so, dreads it more than ever. True godliness does not lie here. It consists, rather, of a pure and true zeal which loves God as a real Father and looks up to him as a real Lord; it embraces his righteousness and detests offending him more than it does dying.

And all those who have this zeal do not set about rashly fabricating a god in line with their own wishes. Instead they seek the knowledge of the true God from God himself, and do not conceive of him as being different from what he reveals himself to be and what he makes known to them.

3. *What we must know about God*

Since God's majesty is intrinsically above and beyond the power of human understanding, and just cannot be grasped by it, we must adore its loftiness rather than scrutinise it, so as not to be entirely overwhelmed by such brightness.

This is why we must seek and consider God in his works which, for this reason, the Scripture calls *manifestations of what is invisible* (*Rom.* 1:19–20; *Heb.* 11:1) because these works portray to us what we could not otherwise know of the Lord.

We are not talking here about empty and frivolous speculations which keep our minds in a state of uncertainty, but of something which it is essential for us to know—something which does us good, and which establishes in us a true and solid piety, that is, faith mixed with fear.

In looking at this universe, then, we gaze upon the immortality of our God. It is this immortality which gives rise to the beginning and origin of everything which exists. We gaze upon his power which has created such a vast system and now sustains it. We gaze upon his wisdom which has brought into being such a great and varied array of creatures, and rules them in a finely-balanced and ordered way. We gaze upon his goodness which was the very reason why all these things were created and continue to exist. We gaze upon his justice which displays itself in a marvellous way in the protection of good people, and in the punishment of bad ones. We gaze upon his mercy which so gently puts up with our sins, in order that it might call on us to put our lives straight.

Indeed, it is so very necessary for us to be plentifully taught about God, and we really ought to let the universe do it for us. And it would do, if it were not for the fact that our coarse insensitivity is blind to such a great light. But it is not only in being blind that we sin. Such is our waywardness that, when it considers God's works, there is nothing that it does not perceive in an evil and perverse sense. It turns upside down all the heavenly wisdom which otherwise shines so clearly there.

We therefore have to come to the Word of God

where, through his works, God is very well described to us. There his works are not evaluated according to the perversity of our judgment, but by the standard of eternal truth. We learn there that our God, who is the only God, and who is eternal, is the spring and fountain of all life, righteousness, wisdom, strength, goodness and mercy. Everything which is good, with no exception whatever, comes from him alone. And so it is that all praise should rightly return to him.

And although all these things appear clearly in each part of heaven and earth, it is ultimately in the Word of God that we always truly understand what is the main goal towards which they are heading, what their value is and in what sense we should understand them. Then we go down deep inside ourselves and consider how the Lord displays in us his life, wisdom and power, and how he exercises towards us his justice, kindness and goodness.

4. *What we must know about man*

At the beginning, man was formed in the image and resemblance of God, so that he might admire his Maker in the dignity with which God had so nobly invested him, and might honour him with appropriate thankfulness.

But man, trusting in the enormous excellence of his nature, and forgetting where it had come from and by whom it continued to exist, endeavoured to exalt himself apart from the Lord. He therefore had to be stripped of all God's gifts, on which he foolishly prided himself, so that, divested and deprived of all glory, he might know this God who had so enriched him by his generous gifts, and whom he had dared to despise.

This is why all of us—who owe our origin to Adam's descendants, and in whom this resemblance to God is erased—are flesh born from flesh. For although we are made up of a soul and a body, we never feel anything but the flesh. The result is that whatever aspect of man we look at, it is impossible for us to see anything other than what is impure, irreverent, and abominable to God. For man's wisdom, blinded and steeped in numberless errors, sets itself against God's wisdom; the will, wicked and full of corrupt affections, hates God's justice more than anything; and human strength, incapable of any good deed whatever, is furiously inclined towards iniquity.

5. Free will

Scripture often asserts that man is the slave of sin. What it means is that his mind is so far removed from God's righteousness that he thinks of, deeply desires and undertakes nothing that is not evil, perverse, iniquitous and sullied; for the heart, having drunk its fill of sin's venom, can emit nothing but sin's fruits.

However, we must not think that there is some violent necessity driving man to sin. He sins with the full agreement of his own will, and he does it eagerly and in line with his own inclinations.

The corruption of his heart means that man has a very strong and continuing hatred of the whole of God's righteousness. In addition, he is devoted to every kind of evil. Because of this he is said not to have the free power of choosing between good and evil—which is called free will.

6. *Sin and death*

In Scripture, sin means both that perversity of human nature which is the source of every vice, and the evil desires which are born from it, and also the unjust and shameful acts which spring from these desires : murders, thefts, adulteries and other things of this sort.

We then, sinners from our mother's womb, are all born exposed to the anger and retribution of God.

Having become adults, we pile up on ourselves—ever more heavily—the judgment of God.

Finally, throughout the whole of our life, we accelerate towards death.

For there is no doubt that God's righteousness finds all iniquity loathsome. What, then, can we expect from the face of God—we miserable people who are loaded down with such a weight of sin, and polluted by numberless impurities—except that his righteous indignation will most certainly put us to shame?

It is necessary for us to know this truth, although it strikes man down with terror and crushes him with despair. Stripped of our own righteousness, drawn away from all trust in our own strength, turned away from all hope of ever having life, the understanding of our own poverty, misery and disgrace thus teaches us to prostrate ourselves before the Lord. By recognising our iniquity, powerlessness and utter ruin, we learn to give him all glory for his holiness, power and salvation.

7. *How we are brought to salvation and life*

This knowledge of ourselves, if it has really entered into our hearts, shows us our nothingness, and by it, the way into the true knowledge of God is made easy for us. And the God of whom we are speaking has already opened for us, as it were, a first door into his kingdom when he has destroyed these two awful plagues: a sense of security when faced with his retribution, and false confidence in ourselves. For it is then that we begin to lift up our eyes to heaven, eyes that were previously fixed and set upon the earth. And we, who used to find our rest in ourselves, yearn for the Lord.

And also, on the other hand, although our iniquity deserves something quite different, this merciful Father, in his incredible goodness, then voluntarily reveals himself to us who are thus afflicted and terror-stricken. And by such means, which he knows to be helpful to us in our weakness, he calls us back from error to the right road, from death to life, from ruin to salvation, from the realm of the devil to his own realm.

To all those whom he pleases to re-establish as heirs to eternal life the Lord has ordained, as a first step, that they should be distressed in their conscience, bent beneath the weight of their sins, and moved to live in his fear. To begin with, therefore, he sets out his Law, which is what brings us to this state.

2

The Law
of the Lord

In the Law of God a truly perfect standard of righteousness is given to us which, with good reason, can be called the eternal will of the Lord, for there, fully and clearly contained in two Tables, is all that he requires of us.

In the first Table, he has laid down for us, in just a few commandments, what is the service of his majesty which pleases him. In the second Table, he tells us what are the duties of charity which are due to our neighbour.

Let us listen to the Law, then, and we shall see afterwards what doctrine we ought to draw from it and, similarly, what fruit we ought to gather from it.

1. *The Ten Commandments*

The First Commandment

I am the Lord, your God, who rescued you from the land of Egypt and from the house of slavery. You shall have no other gods before my face.

The first part of this commandment is like a preface to the whole Law. For, when he affirms that he is *the Lord, our God*, God declares himself to be the one who has the right to command, and to whose commandment obedience is due. So it is that he says through his prophet: 'If I am a Father, where is the love [which is due to me]? If I am Lord, where is the reverential fear [which is due to me]?' (*Mal.* 1:6).

In a similar way he reminds us of his blessings, making it obvious how ungrateful we are if we do not obey his voice. For it is by the same goodness through which he *rescued* the Jewish people *from the slavery* of Egypt that he also delivers all his servants from the Egypt which continues to exist, that is, from the power of sin.

His prohibition of having *other gods* means that we must not attribute anything which is proper to God to any other being at all.

And he adds *before my face*, declaring in this way that he wishes to be acknowledged as God, not just by an outward confession, but in pure truth from the depth of the heart.

Now, these are the things which are proper to God alone and which cannot be transferred to another without robbing him: that we should worship only him, that we should rely on him with our whole trust and with our whole hope, that we should acknowledge that it is from him that whatever is good and holy comes, and that we should praise him for all goodness and holiness.

The Second Commandment

You shall not make for yourself any image nor any resemblance of the things which are in the heaven above, or on the earth here below, or in the waters which are under the earth. You shall not bow your head to them nor shall you honour them.

Just as by the previous commandment he declared himself to be the only God, so now he states who he is and how he must be served and honoured.

He forbids, then, that we should have in mind any *resemblance* to him. He gives the reason for this in Deuteronomy 4: 15–19 and in Isaiah 40:18–26, that is, because the Spirit is nothing like the body.

Furthermore, he forbids in religion that we should honour *any image*.

So let us learn from this commandment that the service and honour of God are spiritual, for, as he is Spirit, it follows that he desires to be served and honoured in spirit and in truth (*John* 4:24).

He then adds a terrible threat by which he declares how very seriously the trangression of this commandment offends him : *For I am the Lord, your God, powerful, jealous, visiting the iniquity of the fathers on the children until the third and fourth generation in those who hate me, and extending mercy to a thousand generations towards those who love me and keep my commandments.*

It is as if he were saying that he is the only one to whom we must cling and that he cannot tolerate any companion god; and even that he will avenge his majesty and his glory if anyone transfers them to images or anything else; and that not only once, but on fathers, children and nephews, that is, on all – so many as there shall be – who will imitate the ungodliness of their fathers. In the same way he is saying that he will show his mercy and kindness to those who love him and keep his Law. And he declares to us the grandeur of his mercy in that he extends it to a thousand generations, while he assigns only four generations to his vengeance.

The Third Commandment

You shall not take the Name of the Lord in vain, for the Lord will not consider as innocent the person who will have taken the Name of the Lord, his God, in vain.

Here he forbids us to misuse his holy and sacred Name in oaths intended to confirm vain things or lies, because oaths must not serve our pleasure or gratification. They are to serve a just necessity, when the glory of God has to be maintained, or when it is necessary to affirm something which tends to edification.

And he absolutely forbids that we should sully his holy and sacred Name in any way at all. Rather, we must take his Name upon our lips with reverence and with all dignity, as his holiness requires. This is true whether we are taking an oath or in any other statement which contains a reference to him.

And since it is mainly by invoking it that people use this Name, let us understand what sort of invocation is commanded here.

Finally, he here announces a punishment, that those who will have profaned the holiness of his Name by the abusive use of it, and by other blasphemies, may not think that they will be able to escape from his retribution.

The Fourth Commandment

Remember the day of rest in order to sanctify it. You shall work six days and do all your work. The seventh day is the rest of the Lord, your God. You shall not do any work, neither you, nor your son, nor your daughter, nor your male servant, nor your female servant, nor your livestock, nor the foreigner who is within your

*doors. For in six days God made the heavens, the earth,
the sea, and all the things which are in them, and on
the seventh day he rested. This is why he blessed the
day of rest and sanctified it.*

We see that there were three reasons behind the
giving of this commandment.

For firstly, by means of the rest of the seventh day,
the Lord wished to represent to the people of Israel
the spiritual rest by which believers must cease from
their own works in order to let the Lord do his work
in them.

Secondly, he wished that there should be established
a definite day in which believers might assemble to
hear his Law and engage in worshipping him.

Thirdly, he wished that a day of rest might be giv-
en to servants and to those who live under the power
of others, that they might have some break in their
labour. But this is rather a consequence than a
principal reason.

As for the first reason, there is no doubt that it came
to an end in Christ: for he is the Truth whose presence
causes all figures to vanish, and he is the Reality at
whose coming all shadows are abandoned. So it is that
St Paul affirms that the sabbath was the shadow of a
future reality (*Col.* 2:16). He declares the same truth
elsewhere when, in Romans 6, he teaches us that we
are buried with Christ, in order that by his death we
may die to the corruption of our flesh (*Rom.* 6:6–7).
And this does not happen in one day, but throughout

our life until, entirely dead to ourselves, we are filled with the life of God. Hence, Christians must have nothing to do with the superstitious observance of days.

These last two reasons cannot be numbered among the shadows of old, but belong equally to all ages. Because of this, although the sabbath is abrogated, it still happens amongst us that we agree to meet on certain days to hear the Word of God, to break the mystic bread of the Supper, and to pray publicly. For such is our weakness that it is impossible for such assemblies to take place every day of the week. It is also essential that servants and workers should be able to rest from their labour.

So it is that the day the Jews observed has been taken away (which was helpful in eliminating superstition), and another day has been set aside for this purpose (which was necessary for securing and maintaining order and peace in the Church).

The truth, then, was given to the Jews through figures, but to us it is revealed without any shadow at all:

Firstly, that in the whole of our life we might meditate on a perpetual sabbath rest from our works, so that the Lord might operate in us by his Spirit;

Secondly, that we might maintain the legitimate order of the Church in order to listen to the Word of God, to receive the Sacraments, and to pray publicly;

Thirdly, that we should not inhumanly oppress with work those who are subject to us.

The Fifth Commandment

Honour your father and your mother so that your days might be extended on the land which the Lord, your God, will give you.

By this commandment we are instructed to exercise piety towards our fathers and mothers and, in the same way, to those who are placed over us, such as princes and civil rulers. That is to say, that we are to show them respect, obedience and thankfulness, and to render to them every service possible. For it is the Lord's will that we should act like this to those who have given us life. And it is of little importance whether they are worthy or unworthy of this honour for, whatever they may be, they have been given to us as father and mother by the Lord, who has willed that we should honour them.

But there is something else we must notice in passing: we are not commanded to obey them except in God. So we must not transgress the Law of the Lord just to please them, for if they command us to do anything against God, on this point we must not consider them as father and mother, but as strangers who wish to pull us away from obedience to our true Father.

This fifth commandment is the first one that carries a promise, as St Paul says in Ephesians 6:2. In promising the blessing of this present life to children who will have served and honoured their fathers and mothers by an appropriate observance of this commandment, the Lord is also declaring that a curse most certainly awaits those who rebel against them and are disobedient to them.

The Sixth Commandment

You shall not kill.

Here we are forbidden all violence and attack, and in general every offence which might wound the body of our neighbour.

For if we recall that man is made in the image of God, we must consider our neighbour to be holy and sacred, in such a way that it is impossible to abuse him without also abusing the image of God which is in him.

The Seventh Commandment

You shall not be dissolute.

Here the Lord forbids us any kind of sexual impropriety or immodesty. For it is by the law of marriage alone that the Lord has joined man to woman, and, as this union is sealed by his authority, he has also sanctified it by his blessing. It follows that every other form of union apart from marriage is cursed before him.

Those, then, who do not have the gift of remaining

chaste (a special gift which is not within everyone's power) must provide for the ungovernable appetite of their flesh by the honest remedy of marriage. For marriage is honourable among all, but God will condemn debauched people and adulterers (*Heb.* 13:4).

The Eighth Commandment

You shall not steal.

Here, generally, we are forbidden and prohibited from seizing other people's goods. For the Lord wishes that his people should have nothing whatever to do with all robberies by which the weak are overwhelmed and oppressed, as well as all kinds of fraud by which the innocence of simple people is taken advantage of.

If, then, we wish to keep our hands pure, and innocent of theft, we must refrain from all forms of cunning and trickery as much as from violent robberies.

The Ninth Commandment

You shall not state any false evidence against your neighbour.

Here the Lord condemns all evil-speaking and insults by which the good reputation of our brother is tarnished, and all lies which would cause him to be wounded in any way at all.

For since a good name is more precious than any treasure anywhere, we are no less damaged by being robbed of the integrity of our good reputation than we would be if we were stripped of our goods. And often one is as successful in carrying off a brother's goods through giving false witness, as by seizing them with one's hands.

Hence, just as the previous commandment ties the hands, so this one ties the tongue.

The Tenth Commandment

You shall not covet your neighbour's house and you shall not desire his wife, nor his male servant, nor his female servant, nor his ox, nor his ass, nor anything which belongs to him.

By these words the Lord puts, as it were, a tight rein on all our strong desires which go beyond the limits set by love for others. All the other commandments prohibit committing acts against the rule of love, but this one forbids even conceiving them in the heart.

So this commandment condemns hatred, envy and ill-will, just as murder was condemned earlier. Obscene sentiment and inner impurity of heart are as much forbidden as depraved behaviour. Just as, before, graspingness and cunning were prohibited, so now is greed for riches. Where previously malicious talk was banned, so now spite itself is curbed.

We see how much this commandment is intended

to be of general application, and how far and wide its extent is. For the Lord requires us to love our brothers with a marvellous affection which burns intensely like a flame. He wants this affection to be untroubled by the slightest evil desire threatening the welfare and advancement of our neighbour.

The sum and substance of this commandment, then, is that we are to be so lovingly disposed towards others that we will not be even slightly affected by any strong desire in conflict with the law of love, and that we will be both ready and very willing to give to each person what is his. And for each person we must consider this to be what the duty of our position requires us to give to him.

2. *The Law summarised*

When he taught that the whole Law is contained in two articles, our Lord Jesus Christ declared to us clearly enough what is the real purpose of all the commandments of the Law.

The first article is that we should love the Lord, our God, with all our heart, with all our soul and with all our strength.

The second article is that we should love our neighbour as much as we love ourself.

And he has taken this interpretation from the Law itself, for the first part is found in Deuteronomy 6:5, and we see the other in Leviticus 19:18.

3. What comes to us from the Law alone

There, then, is the standard and pattern of a holy and righteous life, and even a most perfect picture of righteousness; so that if someone expresses the Law of God in his life, he will not lack before the Lord anything of what is required of perfection.

To bear this out, God promises to those who will have carried out his Law not only the great blessings of the present life which are referred to in Leviticus 26:3–18 and Deuteronomy 28:1–14, but also the reward of eternal life (*Lev.* 18:5)

On the other hand, God announces the retribution of eternal death for those who will not have accomplished by their deeds all that is commanded in this Law (*Deut.* 28:15–68). Also Moses, having made the Law known, takes heaven and earth to witness that he has just put before the people good and evil, life and death (*Deut.* 30:19–20).

But although the Law shows the path to life, yet we have to see how it can benefit us. Of course, if our will were fully trained and disposed to obey God's will, just to know the Law would be more than enough to save us. As it is, however, our carnal and corrupt nature fights all the time, and in every way, against the spiritual Law of God. The teaching of this Law does not improve our nature in any way at all. So it is that this same Law (which was given for salvation if it had found hearers who were good and capable of keeping it) turns into something which results in sin and death.

For since we are all convicted of being transgressors of the Law, the more clearly the Law reveals to us the righteousness of God, the more clearly, on the other hand, it uncovers our unrighteousness.

Consequently, the more the Law catches us going further into transgression, the heavier will be the judgment of God of which it finds us guilty. The promise of eternal life being removed, all that remains for us is the curse which, by the Law, falls on us all.

4. *The Law is a step in coming to Christ*

The evidence given by the Law proves the unrighteousness and transgression of all of us. Its purpose in this, however, is not that we might fall into despair nor, being totally discouraged, that we should founder in ruin.

Admittedly, the apostle testifies that we are all condemned by the Law's judgment, so that every mouth may be closed and the entire world found guilty before God (*Rom.* 3:19). However, he himself teaches elsewhere that God has imprisoned all men under the power of unbelief, not in order to ruin them or let them perish, but that he might have mercy on all (*Rom.* 11:32).

Having then used the Law to tell us of our weakness and impurity, the Lord comforts us through trust in his power and mercy. And it is in Christ, his Son, that he reveals himself as being benevolent and favourably disposed to us.

In the Law, God appears only as the rewarder of perfect righteousness —of which we are completely bereft—and, on the other hand, as the upright and strict Judge of sins. Yet, in Christ, his face is full of grace and gentleness, and shines on miserable, unworthy sinners. For this is the admirable display of his infinite love that he gave to us: he delivered up his own Son for us and, in him, opened to us all the treasures of his mercy and goodness.

3

Faith

1. We lay hold of Christ by faith

The merciful Father offers us his Son through the Word of the gospel. And it is by faith that we embrace him and acknowledge him as given to us.

It is true that the Word of the gospel calls all men to participate in Christ, but many, blinded and hardened by unbelief, spurn such extraordinary grace. Only believers, then, enjoy Christ; only they receive him as sent to them. He is given to them, and they do not reject him. They are called by him, and they follow him.

2. Election and predestination

In looking at this difference between believers and unbelievers we must necessarily consider the great secret of God's counsel: for the seed of God's Word takes root and bears fruit only in those whom the Lord, by his eternal election, has predestined to be his children and heirs of the heavenly kingdom.

To all the others who (by the same counsel of God, before the foundation of the world) are rejected, the clear and plain preaching of the truth can be nothing but an odour of death which leads to death.

Now the reason why the Lord treats some mercifully and exercises the rigour of his judgment towards others we must leave to be known by him alone, for he, with very good intentions, has wished that it should be hidden from us all. The coarse insensitivity of our mind would not be able to bear such a great light; nor would our smallness be able to understand such great wisdom.

In fact, all those who will try to rise to such a height, being unwilling to hold in check the foolhardiness of their spirit, will experience the truth of what Solomon says: that he who desires to investigate the majesty of God will be crushed by his glory (*Prov.* 25:2).

It is enough for us to have decided this in our hearts: that this dealing of the Lord, although hidden from us, is nonetheless holy and just. For if God wanted to ruin all humanity, he would have the right to do it. And in those whom he rescues from perdition, one can contemplate nothing but his sovereign goodness.

Let us recognise, then, that the elect are the recipients of his mercy—and that is the right way to describe them!—and that the reprobate are the recipients of his anger, which, after all, is only just (*Rom.* 9:22–23). From our consideration of both, let us draw solid reasons for extolling his glory.

On the other hand, let us not seek (like so many) to penetrate as far as heaven and to enquire what God, from his eternity, has decided to do with us—and all this with a view to confirming the certainty of our salvation. Such a quest can serve only to stir up miserable anguish and upset in us. Rather, let us be content with the testimony by which he has sufficiently and amply assured us of this certainty. It is in Christ that all those who have been preordained to life have been elected, and this took place even before the foundations of the world had been laid. Similarly, it is in Christ that the pledge of our election is presented to us, if we receive and embrace him by faith.

For what is it that we are looking for in election, if it is not that we might be partakers of eternal life? And we have this life in Christ, he who was Life from the beginning, and who is set before us as Life, so that all who believe in him should not perish but enjoy eternal life (*John* 3:16).

In possessing Christ by faith, we also possess eternal life in him. This being so, we have no reason to enquire any further concerning the eternal counsel of God. For Christ is not only a mirror by which the will of God is presented to us, but he is a pledge by which it is sealed to us and endorsed.

3. What true faith is

We must not think that Christian faith is a pure and simple knowledge of God, or an understanding of the

Scripture, which flutters about in the brain without touching the heart. That is the opinion we normally hold of things which are validated for us by some reason which sounds probable.

Christian faith is, rather, a firm and solid assurance of the heart, by which we cling securely to the mercy of God which is promised to us through the gospel.

Thus the definition of faith must be taken from what underlies the promise. And faith is so very much built on this foundation that it would immediately collapse, or, rather, completely vanish, if this foundation were taken away.

Hence when the Lord presents to us his mercy through the promise of the gospel, if we entrust ourselves to him who made the promise, and if we do this with certainty and without any hesitation, it is then that we lay hold of his Word by faith.

And this definition is no different from that of the apostle, who teaches us that faith is the reality of the things we hope for, the expression of what we do not see (*Heb.* 11:1). By that, the apostle means a sure and certain possession of the things God promises, and a manifestation of things which are not physically visible—that is to say, the eternal life which we hope to have by reason of our trust in this divine generosity which is given to us through the gospel.

Now since all God's promises are confirmed in Christ and, so to speak, kept and accomplished in him, it is clear that Christ is indisputably the perpetual object of faith. And it is in that object that faith contemplates all the riches of divine mercy.

4. *Faith is a gift of God*

If we honestly consider within ourselves how very blind our thought is when faced with the heavenly secrets of God, and how very unfaithful our heart is in everything, we shall not doubt that faith is infinitely beyond all the power of our nature and that it is an extraordinary and precious gift of God. For as St Paul says, 'Nobody knows the things of man, except for the spirit of man which is in him; and nobody knows the things of God except the Spirit of God' (*1 Cor.* 2:11). If the truth of God wavers in us, even in things that our eye sees, how could it be firm and stable in things which the Lord promises our eye cannot see nor our intelligence grasp?

It is clear, then, that faith is an illumination from the Holy Spirit which enlightens our minds and strengthens our hearts; it settles us in this assurance — that the truth of God is so certain that he will accomplish everything that his holy Word has promised he will do.

This is why the Holy Spirit is described as being a guarantee which confirms in our hearts the certainty of divine truth, and as a seal sealing our hearts while we look forward to the day of the Lord (*2 Cor.* 1:22; *Eph.* 1:13). The Holy Spirit witnesses to our spirit that God is our Father and that we are his children (*Rom.* 8:15–16).

5. We are justified in Christ by faith

As Christ is the permanent object of faith, we cannot know what we receive by faith except by looking to him. Now he has been given to us by the Father in order that we may obtain in him eternal life. Jesus said, 'Eternal life is that they might know you—you, the only true God, and he whom you have sent, Jesus Christ' (*John* 17:3); and again, 'He who believes in me will live, even if he should die' (*John* 11:25).

However, for this to happen, we who are polluted by sin must be purified in him, because nothing impure will enter the kingdom of God. This is why we have to participate in him, so that we, who are sinners in ourselves, may through his righteousness be considered just before God's throne. In this way, being stripped of our own righteousness, we are clothed with the righteousness of Christ; and being unjust by our deeds, we are justified by the faithfulness of Christ.

For we are said to be justified by faith, not because we receive within ourselves any righteousness whatever, but because the righteousness of Christ is credited to us, as if it were really ours; while our own wickedness is not imputed to us. The outcome is that it is possible, in a word, to truly call this righteousness the remission of sins. This is what the apostle so clearly declares in often comparing the righteousness of works to that of faith, and in declaring that the one is destroyed by the other (*Rom.* 10:3–8; *Phil.* 3:9).

In studying *The Apostles' Creed*—which lays out in

order all the realities on which our faith is based and on which it stands—we shall see how Christ has earned this righteousness for us, and what it consists of.

6. We are sanctified by faith so that we might obey the Law

Christ, by his righteousness, intercedes for us before the Father, so that we might be declared righteous, he being our advocate. In just the same way, by making us participants in his Spirit, he sanctifies us, in order to make us pure and innocent. For the Spirit of the Lord came upon him without measure—the Spirit of wisdom, of understanding, of counsel, of strength, of knowledge, and of the fear of the Lord—in order that we might all draw from his fulness and receive grace from the grace given to him (cf. *John* 1:16)

Those, then, who boast of their Christian faith while being at the same time entirely without the Spirit's sanctification, deceive themselves. For the Scripture teaches that Christ has not only been made righteousness for us, but also sanctification. As a result, we cannot receive his righteousness by faith without embracing at the same time that sanctification. The Lord, by that covenant which he made with us in Christ, promises that he will both take away our sins and write his Law in our hearts (*Jer.* 31:31–34; *Heb.* 8:6–12 and 10:11–18).

Obedience to the Law is not, then, a work within our power to accomplish. The power to accomplish this work comes from the Spirit who cleanses our hearts from their corruption, and softens them to be obedient to righteousness.

Now the Law is of no use at all for Christians, outside of faith. In former days the outward teaching of the Law did nothing but accuse us of weakness and transgression. But since the Lord has engraved a love for his righteousness in our hearts, the Law is a guiding lamp to keep us from leaving the right road. It is the wisdom which trains us, instructs us and encourages us to become upright. It is our rule, and it will not tolerate being destroyed by wrongful liberty.

7. Repentance and the new birth

It is now easy for us to understand why repentance is always joined to Christian faith, and why the Lord asserts that no one can enter the kingdom of heaven without being born again (*John* 3:3).

Repentance is that turning round by which, leaving behind the perversity of this world, we come back on to the Lord's path. And seeing that Christ is no minister of sin, if he cleanses us from the stains of sin and clothes us with participation in his righteousness, it is not so that we might then profane such great grace with new offences. It is, rather, that we might dedicate the future course of our life to the glory of the Father who has adopted us as his children.

The coming about of this repentance depends on our new birth and comprises two aspects: the putting to death of our flesh (that is to say, of our inborn corruption) and the spiritual coming to life by which human nature is restored to uprightness.

Throughout our life, then, we are to reflect on the fact that we are dead to sin and to ourselves, in order to live for Christ and his righteousness. And seeing that this process of rebirth is never completed as long as we are the prisoners of this mortal body, we should be careful to continue repenting until we die.

8. *The connection between the righteousness of good works and that of faith*

There is no doubt that good works which proceed from a purified conscience are pleasing to God. Recognising in us his own righteousness, he can only approve and prize it.

We must however be very careful not to be carried away by a worthless trust in good works to the point of forgetting that we are justified only by faith in Christ. For before God, there is no righteousness through works except that which corresponds to his own righteousness. The person who wants to be justified by works, then, must do more than produce just a few good deeds. He must bring with him perfect obedience to the Law. And those who have outstripped all others and have progressed the most in the Law of the Lord are still very far from this perfect obedience.

Moreover, even supposing that the righteousness of God should content itself with a single good work, the

Lord would not find in his saints this one good work done in such a way that he would praise it as righteous. For, although this may seem astonishing, it is indisputably true that there is not a single good work springing from us which is entirely perfect and not soiled by some stain or other.

This explains why we who are sinners and sullied by numerous stains of sin must be justified by something outside of ourselves. We need Christ, then, all the time, so that his perfection may cover our imperfection, his purity may wash away our stains, his obedience may wipe out our disobedience, and, finally, that his righteousness might be freely put to our account—and all this without any consideration of our works, whose value cannot be sustained before the judgment of God.

But when our stains—which otherwise contaminate our deeds before God—are covered in this way, the Lord no longer sees anything in these acts except complete purity and holiness. This is why he honours these acts with great titles and praises. He calls them righteous and treats them as such. He promises them an enormous reward.

In short, we must conclude that the great value of union with Christ is found not only in the fact that we are freely justified because of it, but also in the fact that our works are considered as righteous and are recompensed with an eternal reward.

9. *The Creed*

We have just explained what we obtain in Christ through faith. Let us now hear what our faith must see and consider in Christ in order for it to be strengthened. This is developed in *the Creed* (as it is called) where we see how Christ has been made by the Father to be wisdom, redemption, life, righteousness and sanctification for us.

The identity of the author or authors of this summary of the faith is of little importance, for it does not contain any human teaching but is derived from very reliable Scripture proofs.

But in order that the belief we profess in the Father, the Son and the Holy Spirit should not trouble anybody, let us first of all speak a little about it.

When we mention by name the Father, the Son and the Holy Spirit, we do not have in mind three Gods, but rather the fact that the Scripture and the experience of being devoted to God show to us, in the single being of God, the Father, the Son and the Holy Spirit. This happens in such a way that we cannot even think of the Father without at the same time having in our minds the Son in whom his living image shines, and the Spirit in whom his power and strength appear.

Let us pause, then, and concentrate all the thought of our heart on one God only; however, let us always contemplate the Father with the Son and his Spirit.

I BELIEVE IN GOD, THE ALMIGHTY FATHER,
CREATOR OF HEAVEN AND EARTH.

These words do not only teach us to believe that God is, but rather to know that he is our God, and to take it as certain that we are numbered with those to whom he promises to be their God and whom he receives as his people.

All power is attributed to him: he directs all things by his providence, rules over them by his will, and guides them by his strength and the power of his hand.

When God is called 'creator of heaven and earth', this means that he perpetually upholds, maintains and gives life to all which he once created.

AND IN JESUS CHRIST,
HIS ONLY SON, OUR LORD.

What we taught earlier, namely, that Christ is the very object of our faith, stands out clearly in these words which present in him every aspect of our salvation.

We call him *Jesus*, using the title with which heavenly revelation honoured him, for he was sent to *save* his people from their sins. For this reason the Scripture declares that 'there is no other name under heaven given among men by which we must be saved' (*Acts* 4:12).

The title of *Christ* signifies that he has fully received

the *anointing* of all the graces of the Holy Spirit (who is symbolised by oil in the Scripture). Without these graces we fall as dry and barren branches. This unction has established him:

Firstly, as King. The Father has constituted him King in order that he might subject to himself all power in heaven and on earth, so that we ourselves may become kings in him, having dominion over the devil, sin, death and hell.

Secondly, as Priest. This is so that he might give us peace and reconcile us with the Father by his sacrifice, in order that we ourselves might be priests in him, offering to the Father our prayers, our thanksgivings, ourselves and all that we have, seeing that he is our intercessor and mediator.

In addition, he is called *the Son of God,* but not as believers are, who are sons through adoption and only by grace. He is the true and legitimate Son, and consequently the only one, *unique,* in distinction from all others.

He is *our Lord,* not only because of his deity which, from all eternity, is one with that of the Father, but also in that created flesh in which he has been revealed to us.

For, as St Paul says, 'There is but one God, the Father, from whom come all things and for whom we exist, and but one Lord, Jesus Christ, through whom are all things and by whom we exist' (*1 Cor.* 8:6).

WHO WAS CONCEIVED BY THE HOLY SPIRIT, BORN OF THE VIRGIN MARY.

Here we are reminded how the Son of God became *Jesus* for us—that is to say, Saviour—and *Christ*—that is to say, the Anointed One, as King to keep us and as Priest to reconcile us with the Father.

He took our flesh in order that, having become Son of man, he should make us become, with him, sons of God. He clothed himself in our poverty in order to transfer to us his riches. He took upon himself our weakness in order to strengthen us by his power. He assumed our mortal condition so as to give us immortality. He descended to earth to raise us to heaven.

He was *born of the virgin Mary* so as to be recognised as the true son of Abraham and of David, the one who had been promised by both the Law and the prophets. He was a true man, like us in everything, with the single exception of sin. He was tempted in line with all our weaknesses, thus learning to have compassion on them. Nonetheless, he was himself *conceived* in the womb of the Virgin, by the marvellous and inexpressible power *of the Holy Spirit,* so as to be born without being tainted by any fleshly corruption, but sanctified by sovereign purity.

HE SUFFERED UNDER PONTIUS PILATE, WAS CRUCIFIED, DEAD AND BURIED. HE DESCENDED INTO HELL.

These words teach us how he accomplished our redemption, for which he had been born as a mortal man. For by his obedience he wiped out the disobedience of man which was provoking the wrath of God, yielding himself in obedience to his Father right up to his death. In his death, he offered himself as a sacrifice to the Father, so that the Father's justice might once and for all be appeased, in order that all believers might be eternally sanctified, and eternal satisfaction be accomplished. He has shed his holy blood as the price of our redemption, in order that God's anger, inflamed against us, should be extinguished, and that we should be purified from our iniquities.

In this redemption there is nothing that is without mystery.

He suffered under Pontius Pilate, whose verdict condemned him as a criminal and lawbreaker, in order that we, through this condemnation, might be freed and acquitted before the judgment seat of the great Judge.

He was crucified in order to endure on the cross—which was cursed in God's Law—the curse which our sins deserved.

He died in order, by his death, to conquer the death which threatened us, and to swallow it up—that death which otherwise would have swallowed and devoured us all.

He was buried so that we, united to him by the active power of his death, might be buried with our sin and delivered from the power of the devil and of death.

As for the expression *he descended into hell*, this means that he was struck by God and that he endured and felt the horrible rigour of God's judgment, putting himself between God's anger and ourselves, and satisfying God's justice on our behalf. He thus suffered and bore the punishment which our unrighteousness deserved, while there was not the slightest trace of sin in him. Not that the Father was ever incensed against him: for how could he ever have been furious against his beloved Son in whom he found all his joy? And besides, how could the Son have appeased God by his intercession if he had angered him? But he bore the weight of God's anger in the sense that being struck and overcome by the hand of God, he experienced all the expressions of God's fury and retribution, to the point of being moved to cry out in his anguish, 'My God, my God, why have you abandoned me?' (*Matt.* 27:46).

ON THE THIRD DAY HE ROSE AGAIN FROM THE DEAD.
HE ASCENDED INTO HEAVEN
AND IS SEATED AT THE RIGHT HAND OF GOD,
THE ALMIGHTY FATHER.
FROM THERE HE WILL COME TO JUDGE
THE LIVING AND THE DEAD.

By his resurrection we have the unshakeable assurance of obtaining victory over the rule of death. The fact is that he could not be held prisoner by death's chains. By exercising all his power he came out of it, thus breaking in pieces its weapons in such a way that they can no longer strike us mortally.

His *resurrection,* then, is the certain fact, the basis and foundation not only of our own resurrection to come, but also of this present resurrection which enables us to live a new sort of life.

By his *ascension* into heaven he has opened to us the gate of the kingdom of heaven which was closed to everyone in Adam. In fact he has entered into heaven with our human nature, in our name as it were, so that in him we already possess heaven through hope and sit with him in the heavenly realms. And it is for our good that he has entered into God's sanctuary — a sanctuary not made by man's hand. In accordance with his office of eternal priest he has entered there to be our perpetual advocate and mediator.

He is seated at the right hand of the Father. This means, first of all, that he is established, and declared to be, King, Master and Lord over all things in order to keep and sustain us by his power, so that his reign and glory might be our strength, power and glory against the powers of hell.

Secondly, this means that he received all the graces of the Holy Spirit in order to distribute them to those who are faithful to him, and to enrich them with them. Hence, although his body has been taken up to heaven and is no longer here for us to see, yet he does not cease to support his faithful ones with his help and power, and to show to them the evident force of his presence, according to his promise, 'See, I am with you every day until the end of the world' (*Matt.* 28:20).

It follows, finally, that *he will descend from there* on the last day. He will do this visibly, just as he was seen to ascend. He will then appear to all in the incomprehensible majesty of his reign in order *to judge the living and the dead,* (that is to say those whom that day will find still alive, and those who will then be already dead). He will render to all according to their works, just as each one, by his works, will have shown himself to be faithful or unfaithful. It is an extraordinary comfort to us to know that the judgment is committed to the very one whose coming means, for us, nothing but salvation.

I BELIEVE IN THE HOLY SPIRIT.

The fact that we are taught to believe in the Holy Spirit means that we are commanded to expect from him all the blessings which, in Scripture, are promised in him.

By the power of his Spirit, Jesus Christ brings about everything that is good, wherever it may be. By this power he creates, upholds, maintains and gives life to all things. By the same power he justifies, sanctifies, purifies, calls and draws us to himself, that we may obtain salvation.

When the Holy Spirit thus dwells in us, it is he who enlightens us with his light in order that we may learn and fully know the infinite riches which, by divine generosity, we possess in Christ. It is the Spirit who sets our hearts ablaze with the fire of burning love for God and for our neighbour. Every day, and increasingly, it is he who puts to death and destroys the vices of our evil desire, so that if any good works are found in us, they are the fruit and results of his grace. Without him, there would be nothing but darkness in our minds and perversity in our hearts.

I BELIEVE IN THE HOLY AND UNIVERSAL CHURCH,
AND IN THE COMMUNION OF SAINTS.

We have already seen from what source the Church springs. Belief in the Church is put forward here that we might be assured that all the elect are united, by the bond of faith, in one Church, in one community, in one people of God of which Jesus, our Lord, is the guide, prince and head, as of one body; for it is in Christ that believers were elected before the creation of the world to be all brought together in the kingdom of God.

This society is *catholic,* that is to say, universal, because there are not two or three Churches. All God's elect are united and joined together in Christ in such a way that they depend on a single head, grow as in a single body, and are attached one to another by an arrangement similar to that which holds together members of the same body. They have been truly made *one,* because having one and the same faith, hope and love, they derive their life from the same Spirit of God and are called to receive the same inheritance—eternal life.

This society is also *holy*, because all those who are elected by the eternal providence of God to be welcomed as members of the Church, are all sanctified by the Lord and regenerated spiritually.

The words *the communion of saints* explain even more clearly what the Church is: the communion of believers is such that when one of them receives any gift from God, all share in it, although God's granting of the gift may be more particularly directed to one person than to the others. This is just like members of the same body who, in their unity, all have a share in everything they possess, while each one has his particular gifts and their functions remain varied. So, I repeat, all the elect are gathered together and combined into one single body.

We believe both the Church and her communion to be holy, in such a way that, assured by our firm faith in Christ, we are also sure of being members of that Church.

I BELIEVE IN THE REMISSION OF SINS.

It is on the foundation of the remission of sins that our salvation is built and stands. This remission is, in fact, the door to approaching God and the instrument which holds and keeps us in his kingdom.

All the righteousness of believers is embodied in the remission of sins. For this righteousness is not obtained by any merit, but only through the mercy of the Lord.

Weighed down, distressed and bewildered by the consciousness of their sins, believers are cast down by their awareness of God's judgment. Ill at ease with themselves, they groan and labour as if under a heavy burden, and, because of this hatred of sin and this troubled spirit, they put to death their flesh and everything which comes only from themselves.

Christ has himself purchased the remission of sins and paid for it with the price of his own blood, so that we might have it without paying anything. It is in this blood alone that we must seek for cleansing from our sins and for redress for them.

We are therefore taught to believe that through God's generosity, and by the merit of Jesus Christ's intercession, both remission of sins and grace are granted to us who are called and brought into the body of the Church. Remission of sins is not given to us anywhere else or by any other means, for outside the Church and this communion of saints there is no salvation.

I BELIEVE IN THE RESURRECTION OF THE FLESH
AND IN ETERNAL LIFE. AMEN.

Here, first of all, we are taught to look forward to the coming resurrection. By means of the same power which he used to raise his Son from the dead, it will transpire that the Lord will call out of dust and corruption, and into a new life, the flesh of those who will have been touched by death before the great judgment day. Those found alive at that time will pass into a new life, and this will happen through a sudden transformation rather than through the ordinary form of death.

The words *eternal life* are added in order to distinguish between the position of the good and that of the wicked. The resurrection will, in fact, be common to good and bad alike, but will lead to different conditions.

Our resurrection will be such that, raised from corruption into incorruptibility and from mortality into immortality, and being glorified both in our body and soul, the Lord will receive us into eternal blessedness, removed from all possibility of change and corruption.

We will have true and complete perfection of life, light and righteousness, seeing that we will be inseparably united to the Lord, who, like a spring that cannot run dry, contains within himself all fulness.

This blessedness will be the kingdom of God, that kingdom which is filled with all light, joy, power and happiness. These realities are at the moment well beyond men's knowledge. We see them only as in a mirror and in a distorted manner until the day comes when the Lord will grant us to see his glory face to face.

In contrast to this, the condemned and wicked, who will not have sought and honoured God through a true and living faith, will have no share at all in God or his kingdom. They will be thrown with all the demons into immortal death and incorruptible corruption. Excluded from all joy, from all power, and from all the other blessings of the heavenly kingdom, condemned to perpetual darkness and eternal sufferings, they will be gnawed by a worm which shall never die and burned by a fire which shall never be quenched.

10. What hope is

Faith, as we have seen, is an unwavering persuasion of the truth of God which can neither lie nor deceive, and can be neither hollow nor false. Those who have come to this state of certainty wait with similar confidence for God to fulfil his promises. For them, these promises cannot be anything other than truthful.

So it is that hope is nothing less than the firm expectation of the things that faith believes to be truthfully promised by God.

Faith believes God to be truthful: hope waits for him to display his truthfulness at the appropriate time.

Faith believes that God is our Father: hope reckons that he will always act as such towards us.

Faith believes that eternal life has already been given to us: hope waits for the day when it will be revealed.

Faith is the foundation on which hope is built: hope feeds faith and keeps it alive.

And just as no one can expect or hope for anything from God without first believing his promises, in the same way the weakness of our faith (which, weary, must not falter) must be supported and preserved by persevering hope and expectancy.

4

Prayer

1. The necessity of prayer

On the one hand, the man who is rightly instructed in the true faith sees clearly how very poor he is, how totally bereft of all that is good, and how he lacks any possibility at all of saving himself. Hence, if he wants to find a source of help for his beggary, he must go out of himself and look for it elsewhere.

On the other hand, he contemplates the Lord who generously and willingly offers himself in Jesus Christ and, in Christ, opens to him all heavenly treasures. The Lord does this so that the whole of man's faith may apply itself to looking at this beloved Son, that all he expects may depend on this Son, and that all his hope should be built on, and rooted in, this Son.

Therefore man must turn to God in order to ask from him, by prayer, what he has learned to be in him.

To know that God is the Lord, to know that everything good comes from him, to know that he invites us to ask him for what we need, and yet not to call on him and pray to him, is like knowing of a treasure hidden in the earth and, through indifference, to leave it there, without taking the trouble to dig it up.

2. *The meaning of prayer*

Prayer is a form of communication between God and ourselves by which we set before him our desires, our joys, our complaints—in short, all that goes on in our heart. This being so, every time we call on the Lord we should be careful to descend into the depth of our heart and to speak to him from there, and not just with the throat or tongue.

Of course, it is true that the tongue is helpful in prayer, in that it keeps the spirit more attentive as it thinks about God, and also because this part of our body, specially designed to extol God's glory, must be engaged alongside the heart in reflecting on his goodness. Yet the Lord announces through his prophet what punishment awaits those who honour him with their lips while having no will to actually do it—people whose hearts are far from him (*Isa.* 29:13; *Matt.* 15:8).

If true prayer has to be a pure movement of our heart towards God, we must rid ourselves of every thought of our own glory, all notion of our own dignity and all self-confidence. So it is that the prophet exhorts us to pray, not relying on our own righteousness but on the Lord's immense mercy, that he may grant our requests out of love for himself, seeing that we are named with his Name (*Dan.* 9:18).

This awareness that we have of our own extreme need must in no way deter us from approaching God. Prayer has not been instituted that we might arrogantly exalt ourselves before God, nor that we should extol our dignity, but so that we might admit our poverty, groaning like children telling their father about their troubles. Such a way of thinking should, rather, be like a spur, moving us to pray even more.

There are two things which should really stir us up to pray: first of all, God's directive which commands us to pray; and then the promise by which he assures us that we will receive what we ask.

Those who call on God and pray to him receive remarkable comfort, for they know that by praying they are doing something which pleases him. Being sure of the promise, they have, in addition, the certainty of being answered. 'Ask, and you will receive. Knock, and it will be opened to you. Seek, and you will find' (*Matt.* 7:7), says the Lord. And again, 'Call on me in the day of distress; I will deliver you, and you will glorify me' (*Psa.* 50:15).

This last passage points out that there are two sorts of prayer: invocation (or request) and thanksgiving. In request we set out before God what our hearts desire. In thanksgiving we acknowledge the blessings he has given us. And we must make sure that we constantly use both kinds of prayer. This is because we are plagued with such poverty and destitution that even the best of us must sigh and groan continually, and call on the Lord with all humility. On the other hand, the generous gifts which the Lord lavishes upon us in his goodness are so very abundant that, wherever we look, the wonders of his works are seen to be so great, that we always have reason for praise and thanksgiving.

3. The Lord's Prayer

Our merciful Father has not only commanded us to pray and exhorted us to seek him in all circumstances. But as he sees that we still do not know what we have to ask, and what we stand in need of, he has decided to help us in this ignorance and has himself supplied what we were lacking. Through his kindness, therefore, we receive remarkable strengthening, in that he makes us pray, as it were, with his own mouth. This being so, we clearly will not ask him for anything unreasonable, odd, or out of place.

The prayer he has given and prescribed is composed of six petitions. The first three are particularly concerned with the glory of God. When we say them, this is the only thing we should consider; we should have no thought for our own interest. The other three petitions are concerned with ourselves and ask for the things that we need. But the prayer is arranged in such a way, however, that the glory of God for which we ask in the first three petitions (while turning away our thought from all consideration of our own interest) brings our welfare in its wake. On the other hand, in the last three petitions we ask only for those things which are necessary for us to glorify God.

OUR FATHER IN HEAVEN

The first rule of all prayer is that it must be presented to God in the name of Christ, for prayer offered in any other name cannot be pleasing to him.

In calling God *our Father* we are certainly putting forward Christ's name.

No man in the world is worthy of introducing himself to God and of appearing in his sight. To save us from the shame which should rightly have been ours, this good heavenly Father has given us his Son Jesus as mediator and intercessor. Led by Jesus, we can boldly approach him, being completely certain that nothing we ask in the name of this Intercessor will be denied us, for the Father cannot refuse him anything.

God's throne is not only a throne of majesty, but a throne of grace. Through Jesus' name we have boldness to appear openly before that throne, in order both to obtain mercy and to find grace when we need it.

In fact, just as we have the commandment to call on God and the promise that all who do so will be answered, so we also have a definite commandment to call on him in Christ's name and are promised that we will obtain all that we ask in his name (*John* 14:13; 16:23).

It is added that God, our Father, is *in heaven*. This is to draw attention to his inexpressible majesty (which our spirit, because of its ignorance, cannot otherwise grasp), for our eyes know no reality more beautiful and full of grandeur than the sky.

This expression *in heaven* conveys that God is exalted, powerful and beyond comprehension. Now when we hear that, it means, every time God's name is mentioned, that we must lift our thoughts on high, so as not to imagine anything carnal or earthly concerning him, not to measure him by our understanding, and not to make his will fit in with our desires.

1. MAY YOUR NAME BE HALLOWED.

To *name* God is to give him that worship by which men praise him for his qualities, that is, his wisdom, goodness, power, justice, truth and mercy.

We ask, then, that God's majesty might be *hallowed* because of its qualities. This is not, of course, because his majesty is capable in itself of any increase or decrease. But all must revere it as holy; it must be acknowledged and extolled. Whatever God does, his actions must be considered glorious, as they truly are. So then, if God punishes, he must be considered just; if he forgives, he must be considered merciful; if he fulfils his promises, he must be considered truthful. And seeing that his glory is, as it were, engraved in everything, and that it shines there, his praises must resound in every mind and on every tongue.

2. May your reign come.

The reign of God is his guiding and governing of his own people by his Holy Spirit, in order to show them, in all their works, the riches of his generosity and mercy. The reign of God is also his throwing into the abyss and his confounding of the reprobate who are unwilling to submit to his rule, and the throwing down of their accursed arrogance, so that it might be clearly demonstrated that no power can stand against his.

We pray, therefore, that God's reign may come. By this we are praying that the Lord will multiply each day the number of believers who celebrate his glory in all their works, and that he will pour the abundant supply of his graces more profusely upon them, in order to live and reign in them in ever greater measure, until, having perfectly united them to himself, he may fill them entirely.

We are also asking that God, by new and increased numbers, will so cause his light and truth to shine every day that Satan, his lies, and the darkness of his reign, may be scattered and done away with.

When we pray in this way, 'May God's kingdom come', we are asking, finally, for this kingdom to be definitively brought to perfection and completed; we are asking that there should come the disclosure of his judgment—the day when he alone will be exalted and will be all in all, after having gathered his own people and received them into glory, and having demolished and brought down the reign of Satan.

3. MAY YOUR WILL BE DONE ON EARTH
AS IT IS IN HEAVEN.

Here we are asking that God should rule and direct everything on earth in accordance with his good pleasure, just as he does in heaven. We are asking that he will steer everything towards the outcome which seems good to him, making use of all his creatures and subjecting all wills to himself, just as he wishes.

By asking this we renounce all desires of our own, handing over and consecrating to the Lord our every disposition, and praying that he will conduct things not in line with our wishes, but as he will both want and decide.

In this way we are asking not only that he will cause our desires to become ineffectual and unavailing when they are contrary to his will, but that he will create in us new minds and hearts, eradicating ours in such a way that no movement of desire may arise in us except a pure consent to his will.

In short, we are asking that in and of ourselves we may will nothing at all, but that his Spirit may will in us, and that by his inspiration we may learn to love everything which pleases him, and to hate and detest everything which displeases him.

4. GIVE US TODAY OUR DAILY BREAD.

Here, in a general way, we are asking for everything which is helpful in maintaining our existence among the things of this world. We are asking not only for food and clothing, but for everything that God knows we need to be able to eat our bread in peace.

To put it briefly, by this petition we are commending ourselves to the Lord's providence and entrusting ourselves to his care, for him to feed us, look after us and preserve us. For this good Father does not despise having even our body in his keeping and care. In this way he trains us to trust him even in little things, moving us to expect from him everything necessary, even to the last crumb of bread and drop of water.

In saying, 'Give us *today* our daily bread', we are showing that we must desire only what we need from one day to the next, being sure that when our Father has fed us today, he will not fail us tomorrow either.

Even if we are living in abundance today, we must still ask for our *daily* bread, recognising that no means of sustaining existence has any value, except in so far as the Lord, by his blessing, makes it fruitful and beneficial. For what we have in our hands is *ours* only in so far as God allows us to use it hour by hour, and gives us some share in it.

In saying *our* daily bread, God's generosity displays itself even further, making ours what was not due to us by any right.

Finally, in asking that this bread should be *given*, it is made clear that everything which comes to us—even when we seem to have acquired it through our own labour—is a straightforward and free gift from God.

5. CANCEL OUR DEBTS
AS WE CANCEL THOSE OF OUR DEBTORS.

We now ask that forgiveness and remission of sins should be given us, for they are necessary to all men without exception.

And we call our offences debts because the punishment of them is the payment we owe to God, and we could not in any way meet this debt if we were not absolved through this remission, which is a free pardon granted by his mercy.

And we ask that our debts should be *cancelled* as we cancel those of our debtors, in other words, in the same way as we forgive those who have wounded us in any way at all, whether it be that we were hurt by actions or insulted by words.

There is no question here of an added condition, as if, by forgiving others, we ourselves deserved the forgiveness of God. We are talking about a sign which God offers us. It is given to assure us that the Lord as certainly receives us in his mercy as we are certain in our consciences of being merciful to others, our heart being well and truly cleansed from all hate, envy and revenge.

Conversely, by this sign God expels from among those he numbers as his children all who, through inclination to revenge and refusal to forgive, keep their ill-will towards others rooted in their hearts. Let such people not embark on calling upon God as Father, for the ill-feeling which they nurse towards men would then fall on their own heads.

6. DO NOT BRING US INTO TEMPTATION,
BUT DELIVER US FROM THE EVIL ONE.
AMEN.

We are not here asking to be spared from enduring any temptation at all; our need of being woken up, stimulated, and shaken by temptations is too great for that. By having too much peace and quiet we are likely to become sluggish and lazy. The Lord tests his elect every day, instructing them through discredit, poverty, suffering and other kinds of crosses.

But our request is that the Lord will give us, with our temptations, a way out of them, so that we may not be conquered and crushed by them, but, rather, strengthened by God's strength, we may constantly stand fast against all the powers which assail us.

And there is more to it than that. Being taken into God's safe keeping and under his protection, being sanctified by the graces of his Spirit, being ruled by his guidance, we will remain invincible in the face of the devil, death, and all hell's devices. This is what it means to be delivered from the evil one.

* * *

We must note how the Lord wants our prayers to be guided by the rule of love. He does not teach that each one of us should ask what is good for himself without considering his fellows, but instructs us to be as concerned for our brother's welfare as for our own.

4. Persevering in prayer

In closing, we must be careful to notice that we are to have no desire to bind God to any set of circumstances, just as we are taught in this Lord's Prayer not to subject him to any law or to impose on him any condition.

Before making any prayer for ourselves, we first of all say to him, 'May your will be done.' In this way we already submit our will to his. This is so that our will—curbed and restrained, as it were, by a bridle—may not presume to want to order him around, and to put him beneath itself.

With our hearts trained to obey him in this way, if we let ourselves be governed by the good pleasure of divine providence, we will easily learn how to persevere in prayer, and how to wait on the Lord with patience, deferring the fulfilment of our desires to the hour set by his will. We will also be certain, however things may appear to us, that he is always present, and that he will show in his own time that his ears have never been deaf to our prayers, though it seemed to men that he might have despised them.

And if, finally, after a long wait, our minds cannot grasp what is the point of our praying, and do not feel that it leads to anything, our faith will nonetheless make us certain of what our senses cannot perceive—that we have obtained everything that was necessary to us. By faith we shall then possess abundance in want and comfort in grief. In fact, even if we have to go without everything, God will never abandon us, for he cannot disappoint the expectation and patience of those who are his. He, on his own, will take the place of everything, for he contains in himself everything that is good—a fact he will fully reveal in the future.

5

The
Sacraments

1. The necessity of the sacraments

The sacraments have been instituted to exercise our
faith before both God and men.

Before God, they exercise our faith by strengthening it in God's truth. For the Lord knows that it is
helpful to the ignorance of our flesh that he should
present high and heavenly mysteries to us by means of
perceptible realities. This is not to imply that such
qualities are inherent in the nature of the things offered to us in the sacraments. It is, rather, the Word of
the Lord which stamps them with such a meaning. The
promise, contained in the Word, always comes first;
the sign is added to confirm and seal this promise,
and, as it were, to make us more sure of it, for the
Lord sees that this procedure suits our poor learning
capacities. Our faith is so small and weak that unless
it is propped up on all sides and upheld by all availa-
ble means, it is suddenly and totally shaken, troubled

and caused to totter.

Before men, the sacraments exercise our faith, for faith then expresses itself in a public confession and is thus prompted to praise the Lord.

2. *What a sacrament is*

A sacrament is an external sign by which the Lord depicts and bears witness to his good will towards us, in order to support the weakness of our faith.

To put it more briefly and clearly, a sacrament is an expression of the grace of God declared by an external sign.

The Christian church makes use of only two sacraments: Baptism and the Supper.

3. *Baptism*

Baptism has been given to us by God, to help, first, our faith in him, and then our confession of faith before men.

Faith looks at the promise by which the merciful Father offers us communion with his Christ, so that, being clothed with him, we may participate in all that he has.

Baptism particularly represents two things: the cleansing we have obtained through Christ's blood, and the putting to death of our flesh which we have experienced through his death.

The Lord has commanded that his people should be

baptised for the remission of sins (*Matt.* 28:19, *Acts* 2:38). And St Paul teaches that Christ sanctifies by his Word of life, and cleanses by water-baptism, the church of which he is the bridegroom (*Eph.* 5:26). St Paul also shows that we are baptised in Christ's death by being buried in his death with a view to walking in newness of life (*Rom.* 6:4).

This does not mean that the water is the cause, or even the instrument, of cleansing and regeneration, but only that the knowledge of these gifts is received in the sacrament. We are said to receive, obtain and rightfully procure that which we believe to be given by the Lord, whether we are knowing these gifts for the first time, or whether, having already known them, we are being more certainly persuaded of having them.

In the same way, baptism helps our confession before men, for it is a mark by which we publicly declare our intention to be numbered among the people of God, so as to honour and serve him in one and the same religion as all believers.

Since the Lord's covenant with us is first and foremost confirmed by baptism, we also rightly baptise our children, for they share in the eternal covenant by which the Lord promises that he will not only be our God, but also the God of our descendants (*Gen.* 17:6–8).

4. *The Lord's Supper*

The promise accompanying the mystery of the

Supper openly declares why it was instituted and with what aim.

This mystery assures us that the Lord's body was once given for us, in such a way that it is now ours and always will be. It assures us that his blood was once shed for us, in such a way that it will always be ours.

The emblems of this mystery are the bread and wine through which the Lord holds out to us the true communication of his body and blood. We are talking of spiritual communion, which is effected by the bond of the Holy Spirit alone, and which in no way requires a presence enclosed in Christ's flesh through the bread or his blood through the wine. For although Christ, exalted in heaven, has left behind this earthly abode in which we are still pilgrims, yet no distance can dissolve his power by which he feeds his people with himself. Although they are very far from him, by this power he grants them to enjoy a communion with himself which is nonetheless very close.

So it is that in the Supper the Lord gives us teaching which is so certain and unmistakable that we must be assured without doubt that Christ, with all his riches, is there presented to us, no less than if he were placed before our eyes and touched by our hands.

The power and efficacy of Christ are such that, in the Supper, he not only brings to our spirits an assured confidence of eternal life, but he also makes us certain of the immortality of our flesh. For our flesh is already given life by his immortal flesh and, in some way, shares in his immortality.

This is why the body and blood are represented to us by means of bread and wine, so that we learn not only that they are ours, but that they are life and nourishment for us. Thus when we see the bread consecrated as the body of Christ, at that moment we should see this parallel in our minds: as bread feeds and preserves the life of our body, so the body of Christ is the nourishment and protection of our spiritual life. And when the wine is presented to us as an emblem of the blood, we must similarly consider we are receiving from Christ's blood, in a spiritual way, the same benefits that wine brings to the body.

Thus this mystery, in the same way as it teaches us how great is God's liberality towards us, also exhorts us not to be ungrateful towards such manifest generosity, but rather to exalt it with fitting praises and to extol it with thanksgiving.

Finally, this sacrament exhorts us to join with each other in the same sort of unity in which the members of a body, linked as they are, are bound together. For no stronger or sharper spur could be given to move and encourage us to mutual love than this: Christ, in giving himself for us, does not only invite us by his example to give and consecrate ourselves to each other, but makes himself to be shared by all, and also makes us all one in himself.

6

Order in Church and State

1. The pastors of the church and their authority

Since the Lord has willed that both his Word and his sacraments should be dispensed through the ministry of men, it is necessary that there be pastors ordained in the churches, to teach the people pure doctrine, both publicly and privately; to administer the sacraments; and to give to all the good example of a pure and holy life.

Those who despise this discipline and order not only dishonour men, but God himself. Sectarian in spirit, they withdraw from the fellowship of the church, which can in no way hold together without such a ministry. For what the Lord has once attested is of no small importance: that when the pastors he sends are received, it is he himself who is received; and, in the same way, it is he who is rejected when they are rejected (*Matt* 10:40; *Luke* 10:16).

In addition, so that their ministry should be undisputed, pastors have received the striking command to bind and to loose, with the promise attached, 'Whatever you bind on earth will be bound in heaven, and whatever you loose on earth will be loosed in heaven' (*Matt.* 18:18). Christ makes clear elsewhere that to bind means to retain sins, and to loose means to remit them (*John* 20:23). And the apostle declares how unloosing is done, when he teaches that the gospel is 'the power of God to salvation for everyone who believes' (*Rom.* 1:16). And he tells us how binding is done, when he teaches that the apostles are 'ready to punish all disobedience' (2 *Cor.* 10:6). The gospel message, in summary, is that we are slaves of sin and death, that we are loosed and delivered by the redemption which is in Christ Jesus, and that those who do not receive him as redeemer are, as it were, clamped once more in the fetters of a more serious condemnation.

Let us remember, however, that the authority which Scripture attributes to pastors is wholly contained within the limits of the ministry of the Word, for the fact is that Christ has not given this authority to men, but to the Word of which he has made these men servants.

Therefore let ministers of the Word make bold to do all things by that Word which they have been appointed to give out. Let them compel all the powers, celebrities and high-placed people of the world to humble themselves in order to obey the majesty of that Word. By means of that Word, let them give commands to everybody, from the greatest to the least; let them build up Christ's household, demolish Satan's reign, pasture the sheep, kill the wolves, and instruct and encourage the teachable; let them accuse, reprimand and convince the rebellious — but all by the Word of God.

If they should ever turn away from that Word in order to follow the fancies and inventions of their own heads, then they are no longer to be received as pastors; they are, rather, pernicious wolves who are to be chased away! For Christ has laid down that we should not listen to anybody except those who teach us what they have taken from his Word.

2. *Human traditions*

St Paul has given us this general rule for the life of the churches: 'Let everything be done in a seemly and orderly manner' (*1 Cor.* 14:40). We must not then consider as *human traditions* those rulings which serve as restraints to safeguard peace and concord and to uphold order and honesty when Christians gather together. They are totally in harmony with the apostle's rule as long as they are not considered necessary for salvation, nor thought to be part and parcel of the worship of God, nor made the object of any devotion.

On the other hand, we must energetically resist rulings considered essential to the service and honour of God which, known as *spiritual laws*, might be laid down in order to bind consciences. These ordinances do not only destroy the liberty which Christ has secured for us, but they cloud the nature of true religion and do violence to the majesty of God who, all alone, wishes to reign in our consciences by means of his Word.

May this then be firm and settled: all things are ours, but we are Christ's (*1 Cor.* 3:23), and God is served in vain where doctrines are taught which are nothing other than men's commandments (*Matt.* 15:9).

3. Excommunication

Excommunication is the act by which those who are openly immoral people, adulterers, thieves, killers, misers, kidnappers, cheats, quarrellers, gluttons, drunks, rabble-rousers, wasters—if they do not mend their ways after being warned—are rejected from the company of believers, according to God's commandment.

In excommunicating them, the church does not mean to cast them into irreparable ruin and despair, but is condemning their life and standards of behaviour, and is warning them that they will certainly be damned if they do not change for the better.

This discipline is indispensable among believers, because the church is the body of Christ and must not be defiled and contaminated by bumptious and putrid members like these, who dishonour the Head. The saints must not be corrupted and harmed, as happens, by keeping company with wicked people. Besides, the punishment of their malice benefits the wicked themselves, while tolerance would cause them to become more obstinate. In being confounded by shame, they learn to mend their ways.

If wicked people change for the better, the church tenderly receives them afresh both into its fellowship and into the sharing of that unity from which they have been excluded.

In order that no one should obstinately despise the church's judgment, nor be indifferent to having been condemned by the sentence of believers, the Lord attests that the judgment of believers is nothing other than the pronouncement of his own sentence, and that which they have stated on earth is ratified in heaven (*Matt.* 18:15-18). It is the Word of God which gives authority to condemn the perverse, just as it gives authority to receive into favour those who mend their ways.

4. Civil rulers

The Lord has not only declared that he approves the office of civil rulers and that it is pleasing to him, but in addition he has warmly recommended it to us and has honoured the dignity of civil rulers with fine titles of respect.

The Lord affirms that civil rulers are the fruit of his wisdom: 'By me', he says, 'kings reign, and princes order what is right; by me rulers govern, nobles, and all the judges of the earth' (*Prov.* 8:15–16). In the book of Psalms he calls them *gods*, because they do his work (*Psa.* 82:6). It is written elsewhere that they dispense justice for God, and not for men (*Deut.* 1:17). And among the gifts of God St Paul cites those who are over others (*Rom.* 12:8)

It is however in chapter thirteen of the Epistle to the Romans that St Paul gives a longer exposition of this subject, teaching clearly that the authority of civil rulers comes from God, and that they are *ministers of God* to approve those who do good and to dispense God's retribution by punishing those who do evil (*Rom.* 13:1–7).

So princes and civil rulers must not forget whom they are serving when they fulfil their office, and must do nothing unworthy of God's ministers and lieutenants. Their main concern must be to keep the form of public religion truly pure, to direct the life of the people by good laws, and to procure the welfare and tranquillity of their subjects, both in public and in private.

All this can be obtained only by those two things recommended by the prophet as being of prime importance: *justice* and *judgment* (*Jer.* 22:3).

Justice is protecting the innocent. It is supporting them, looking after them and setting them free.

Judgment is resisting the audacity of wicked people, quelling violence and punishing misdeeds.

On the other hand, the duty of subjects is not only to respect and revere those over them but, by prayer, to commend them to the Lord for salvation and prosperity, to submit willingly to their authority, to obey their laws and constitutions, and not to refuse the charges which they impose on them: taxes, tolls, rates and the like, services to the community, conscription and everything similar.

Not only do we owe obedience to civil rulers who exercise their authority both lawfully and in accordance with their duties, but we must also put up with those who tyrannically abuse their power right up until we are freed from their yoke by legitimate law and order. For just as a good prince is a testimony to the divine goodness which intends the salvation of men, so a bad and evil prince is a plague from God for punishing the people's sins. Nonetheless, it must be generally considered certain that authority is given both to one and the other by God himself, and that we cannot resist them without resisting the ordinance of God.

However, when one speaks of the obedience which is due to the authorities there is always one exception to be made: such obedience must not draw us away from obeying him to whose edicts it is right that all the commands of kings must yield. The Lord is the King of kings and everyone must listen to him, and to him alone, once he has opened his mouth, which is so very sacred. It is he who must be listened to above everything else.

Finally, it is in God, and in him alone, that we are made subject to the men who have been placed over us.

And if these men command us to do anything against the Lord, we must not pay any attention to what they say, but must, rather, put into practice this scriptural maxim: 'God is to be obeyed more than men' (*Acts* 4:19).

My people have been taken captive,
because they had no knowledge
(*Isa.* 5:13).

How shall a young man make
his conduct pure? It is by remaining
faithful to your Word
(*Psa.* 119:9)

About the Publisher

THE Banner of Truth Trust originated in 1957 in London. The founders believed that much of the best literature of historic Christianity had been allowed to fall into oblivion and that, under God, its recovery could well lead not only to a strengthening of the church today but to true revival.

Inter-denominational in vision, this publishing work is now international, and our lists include a number of contemporary authors along with classics from the past. The translation of these books into many languages is encouraged.

A monthly magazine, *The Banner of Truth,* is also published and further information will be gladly supplied by either of the offices below or from our website.

THE BANNER OF TRUTH TRUST

3 Murrayfield Road
Edinburgh, EH12 6EL
UK

PO Box 621, Carlisle
Pennsylvania, 17013
USA

www.banneroftruth.co.uk